Mick Manning
Brita Granström

W
FRANKLIN WATTS
LONDON·SYDNEY

Contents

Beside the seaside! 4

Welcome to where the land meets the sea. Build a sandcastle and make your own sand. Well, try . . .

On the beach 6

Look at sand up close. Feel the ripples and create some sandy art.

Kersplash! 8

Discover the power of waves, and how you can use a candlestick to make great wave paintings.

Tides turning 10

Lots of animals live by the sea, but their world is always changing with the rise and fall of the tides . . .

Sea shells 12

Everyone finds empty shells by the sea. But do you know about the animals that once lived inside them? And is it really the sea you hear when you hold a shell to your ear?

Whooshing wind! 14

Become a seabird and feel the wind in your wings! Or listen to it with your very own wind chimes.

Seabirds 16

More seabird activities – from bird-watching to making a seabird mask.

Beach detective 18

Follow the clues in the sand and work out who got to the beach before you . . .

Flotsam and jetsam 20

The strangest things get washed up on the beach – some of them can be the ingredients for a yummy maggot pie!

Under the water 22

The tide leaves pools of water on the beach. What kind of sea creatures might be lurking in them?

Mermaids and pirates 24

Fishermen have some tales to tell about their adventures on the high seas – mermaids, monsters and buried treasure . . .

Seaside safety 26

The seaside is fun but it can be dangerous . . .

Pollution is rubbish! 28

People may love the seaside, but they make a terrible mess of it, too – dumping rubbish and spilling oil . . .

Seaside senses 30

You need to use all your senses to make the most of the seaside!

Useful words 32

Beside the seaside!

We all love to be beside the seaside! What do you think of when you are going there? The beach, the waves? What else?

Make a sandcastle

Next time you go to the beach, build a sandcastle near to the water. How long does it last? What happens when the tide comes in?

In fact, there are so many things to think about and do at the seaside that we've written a whole book about it, starting with something which always make *us* think of the seaside. Sand!

What is sand?

Pick up a handful of sand and you're holding the result of the waves endlessly breaking on the land for years and years and years . . . Waves break up, or erode, lumps of stone and hard sea shells, grinding them up into the tiny grains that make sand!

Earth is known as 'the blue planet' because most of it is covered by the sea.

Look out for 'shark bites' of information in this book.

Silly experiment

1 Take a handful of small pebbles and put it in a plastic drinks bottle with some water . . .

2 Now shake the pebbles up! See how they smash about in the water?

3 You need to shake it for about 1,000 years to make homemade sand . . . Easy, eh? Come on now – keep shaking!

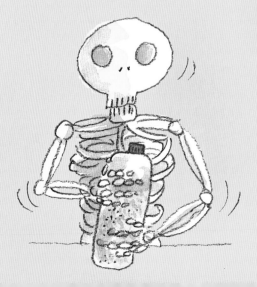

on the beach

Every beach is different. Beaches can be
sandy, muddy, shingly or pebbly. Even sandy
ones vary a lot – the colour and feel of the sand
depend on what has been ground up to make
it. Golden sand may have been made from
yellow sandstone rock. White and pink sand
is mostly made from shells. You sometimes
even get black sand – where there is coal or
black volcanic rock around.

Look closer

Use a magnifying glass to take a closer look
at the sand or shingle from your favourite
beach – or beaches. What do you see?
Is it mainly tiny grains? Or are there
lots of pieces of broken shell and
tiny pebbles?

Make a face

Draw a face in the sand
and use shells, pebbles
and seaweed to
decorate it. Notice how
the waves draw in the
sand, too – they leave
ripple shapes. Animals
and birds also leave
pictures on the beach –
their paw and claw prints!

Sand painting

1 Take a piece of heavy paper or card and paint an underwater picture. Let it dry.

2 Paint PVA glue across the bottom of the picture and sprinkle sand over it to create the seabed (if you haven't got any beach sand, use building sand or sand from a sandpit). You could also stick some pebbles on.

3 When the glue is dry, pin up your picture for everyone to admire.

Sand isn't just good for building sandcastles. People mix it with other things to make bricks and mortar so they can build houses that last for hundreds of years.

Sand ripples

As the waves move up and down the beach, they push up little banks of sand. These ridges look just like ripples of water – and feel bumpy under our feet when we walk over them. Next time you are at the beach, make your own 'ripples' by walking along dragging a piece of driftwood or a long stalk of seaweed behind you.

Kersplash!

Whether they're crashing onto the beach or lapping gently at your toes, waves are beautiful – and never stop coming!

Making waves

It is the pushing force of the wind that makes waves. The stronger the wind, the larger the waves it pushes up.

Make waves in the bath using the lid from a plastic food box as your pushing force – don't get the floor wet, though! Float different plastic boats (or empty plastic tubs) and see how they cope with your wave machine. Do they float or sink? How can you make your waves bigger?

Painting the waves!

You can make a fantastic wave picture using the end of a wax candle and some sea-green watercolour paint.

1 Use the blunt end of the candle to draw big, hilly waves. Put dots for surf where the waves begin to break.

2 Use coloured crayons to draw some seaweed and sea animals.

3 Brush your sea-green paint over the top – and see how your waves magically appear!

People are beginning to use wave power to make clean electricity. Because the waves never stop moving, the supply of electricity never runs out.

9

Tides turning

Tides are caused by an invisible pulling force between the moon, the sun and the earth. This force is called gravity. It makes the sea rise up and down the beach like water slowly slopping up and down in a huge bath!

At the water's edge, birds hunt for worms which live under the damp sand at low tide. The worms come out to feed when the beach is under water.

High tide level ▲

Upper shore

This zone is above the tide but is splashed by spray and may get wet at very high tides or in storms.

Middle shore

This zone is covered and uncovered by the tide twice a day. As the tide goes out, it leaves behind pools of water – and many small sea animals in them.

Make a tidal frieze

Make a frieze of your favourite beach using a sheet of wallpaper, paint or crayons, or even animal magazines.

1 First mark in the sea and waves, then the rocks, sand and land. Maybe include a cliff, some grassy dunes or a promenade.

The tide rises and falls twice every day so the coast is always changing. This creates areas of the seashore known as tidal zones.

The high and low tide level changes with the monthly cycle of the moon. The highest and lowest tides are 'spring' tides. These happen when the moon is full or new, which is when the pull of gravity is strongest.

Fish follow the tide to look for food – including tasty worms! And fishing birds follow them!

Lower shore

This zone is only uncovered at very low tides. It is full of life, including crabs, fish and seaweed.

Shallow sea

Where the sea is shallow, the water is warmer so it is home to the most sea creatures. Dolphins and even small sharks come to feed here.

Level of low tide ▲

2 Add vertical lines to show the tidal zones as in the picture above.

3 Make a list of the different animals that you see at the seaside – crabs, fish, birds, shellfish, seals and dolphins . . .

4 Draw pictures of these animals or cut them out from magazines. Add them to your frieze in the tidal zone you think they come from. Put other seaside things on your frieze, like boats and holiday-makers!

11

Sea shells

Everyone collects empty shells when they go to the seaside. Shells are the 'outside skeleton' of animals called shellfish. The shells protect these animals' soft bodies. After shellfish die, their shells are often washed up on the beach – for us to find!

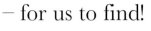

Razors dig themselves deep into the sand.

Mussels grow in tightly packed colonies.

Whelks are scavengers. Some prey on other shellfish.

Barnacles grow on rocks, boats and even other animals' shells.

Scallops can 'swim' by squirting water through their shell.

Crabs have shell over their backs, legs and pincers.

Winkles, like most shellfish, feed on seaweed.

Otter shells live in the same spot all their lives.

Limpets cling tightly to their rocky homes.

Cockles live in sandy beaches – as many as 10,000 in 1 square metre.

Living shells

1 Razor shells have a long 'foot' to pull them through the sand.

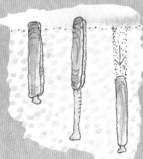

2 The piddock uses its sharp shell to bore into solid rock!

3 Barnacles have to live below the tideline. They feed when they are covered by water.

4 Dog whelks scrape holes in other shellfish and eat them!

Listen to the sea

Never buy shells – the shellfish may have been killed just to sell their shells. Never try to kick a limpet off its rock either; it's cruel.

If you find a large shell, try holding it to your ear. What do you hear? The sea! Well, not really . . . In fact, it's other noises swirling around inside the shell and bouncing off its walls to make a mixed-up echo that sounds like swirling waves.

Listen to different shaped shells or even hold a plastic cup to your ear. What do you hear?

Make a shell necklace

Look for the shells of shellfish eaten by dog whelks – they will have a little hole in them. If you find a few on the beach – or even just one – you can thread them on a string to make a necklace.

13

Whooshing wind!

Seaside weather conditions change very quickly. Sometimes the sun shines but then the wind blows the clouds in. Wind coming in from the sea has nothing to stop it. It whooshes over your head, bringing storms and pushing up the waves into big frothy 'white horses'.

Bird power!

The wind helps birds fly by pushing up against their wings. Make a pair of wings out of cardboard to feel the pushing force of the wind:

1 From corrugated card, cut out two wing shapes that are a bit longer than your arms. Cut a hole in each wing at your arm's length to make a hand grip.

2 Push feathers in the holes along the edges of the corrugated card.

3 Paint a toilet roll tube yellow and tie some elastic on to it so that it fits over your head and nose to make a funny beak!

4 Stand somewhere flat and safe like a beach, park or garden and pretend you are a gull – feel the breeze under your wings, and flap them up and down. Give a good gull squawk: 'Yowk! Yowk!'

DON'T go near a steep drop or a road, or really try to fly. That is very dangerous!

Wind turbines are often placed near the sea. The wind blows their blades around and the turbines change the energy of the wind into electricity.

Test the wind

How windy does it have to be before a kite flies or a wind spinner turns? Notice how even a very gentle breeze will move the spinner around. Another way to test the wind – and to hear it – is to make your own wind-chime stick. You can use it to mark your spot on the beach.

1 Find a good, strong driftwood stick.

2 Tie strips of cloth, plastic, string and seaweed to it. You should be able to find some on the beach.

3 Tie pebbles, shells and twigs to the ends of these strips or attach them separately with string.

4 How windy does it have to be for them to clank together?

Sunburn!

The sun can be dangerous. Too many UV rays damage our skin. The sun can kill small sea animals by drying them out. Animals like worms make a slimy liquid to keep them cool and wet. They burrow into the sand or hide under stones.

1 Suck a jelly sweet until it's sticky and then leave it out in the sun. How long does it take to dry up?

2 Imagine being a sand-worm stuck out in the sun – how long would you last?

Always wear sun protection cream to protect your skin when you are on the beach even if the weather is dull or cloudy.

15

Seabirds

Fish, shellfish, worms, insects, left-over picnics – all these are food for seabirds. Each bird has a beak shape that is specially suited for the food it eats. Do some bird-watching next time you are by the sea.

Diving experts

You often see shags and cormorants drying their wings. This is because of the way they dive for fish.

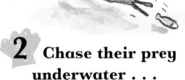

1 They swim along and dive . . .

2 Chase their prey underwater . . .

3 And surface with a fish – if they are lucky!

Make a seabird mask

Make this seabird mask, basing it on your favourite seabird. You can adapt the shape of the beak to match the seabird you choose.

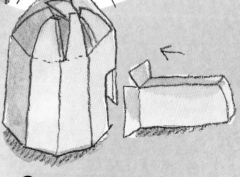

1 Find a cardboard box that fits your head like a hat. Score along the centre of each side as shown. Cut out flaps at the top and a hole for the beak.

2 Squash the head into shape as shown, and make a beak with the left-over card or another box or tube. Attach it to the head.

16

A tern has a forked tail and dives for its food.

A herring gull feeds on anything it can kill or scavenge.

A redshank is named after its long, red legs – perfect for wading.

A dunlin's long beak lets it dig for its food.

A puffin's colourful beak can hold a lot of fish.

A black-headed gull's head is really dark, chocolate brown – and only in the summer.

A guillemot has waterproof feathers and 'flies' under water.

A gannet plunges into the sea from high in the air to catch fish. Its skull is extra strong to take the shock!

3 Tape everything together.

4 Cover the head with newspaper soaked in PVA glue and leave to dry.

5 Paint the head to look like your favourite seabird.

6 Try it on – if you can't see out from underneath, cut out some peepholes.

7 Go and have some seabird fun!

17

Beach detective

Animals (including people!) leave signs behind on the beach: footprints, beak marks, food remains. Try and work out who has been out and about on your beach by studying the clues. Look at these examples first to get you started:

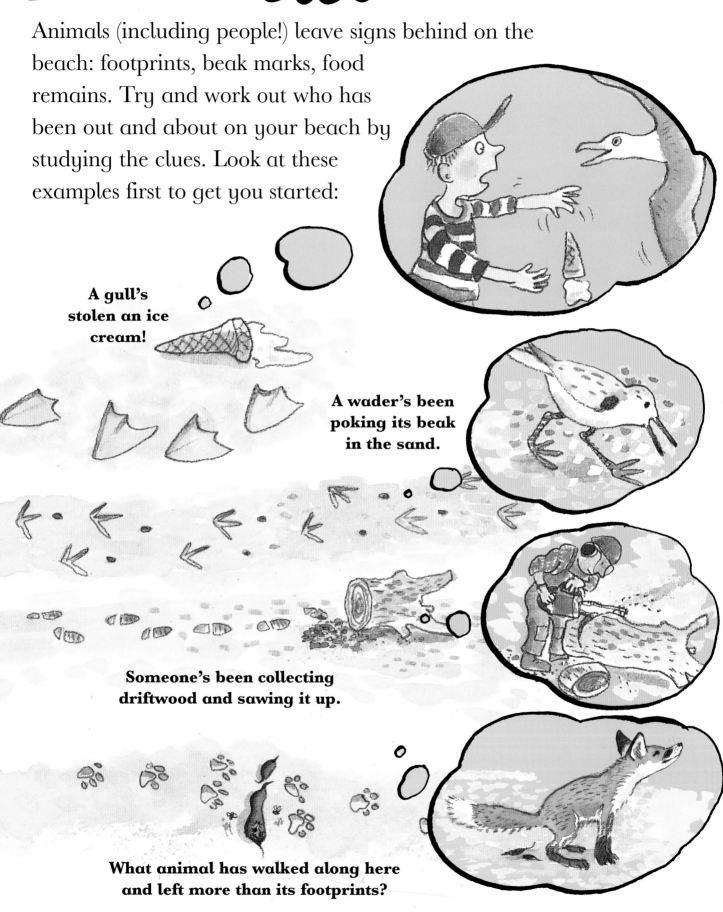

A gull's stolen an ice cream!

A wader's been poking its beak in the sand.

Someone's been collecting driftwood and sawing it up.

What animal has walked along here and left more than its footprints?

Preserving footprints!

You can make a cast of some good clear prints you've found on the beach – or in some mud! You need: paperclips, a long strip of card, plaster of Paris, some rubber gloves, a plastic bowl or bucket and some clean, fresh water.

Prehistoric human footprints have been found on some beaches. The mud they were made in has now turned to stone!

1 Find some good, clear prints. Circle the card around them and clip it together. Push the card down a bit into the sand.

2 Wearing rubber gloves, put the plaster of Paris in the bowl and stir in water until the mixture is like yogurt. Carefully pour this into the card circle.

3 Wait about 30 minutes until the plaster is dry. Remove the card and lift out your cast. Take it home to add to your collection!

A giant bird?

1 Cut out some webbed feet like the one below from thick card (or get an adult to cut you some from plywood).

2 Add straps to tie them to your feet and go off to find some sand. Now you can make scary, giant seabird footprints!

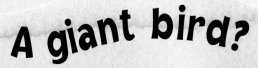

19

Flotsam and jetsam

All the different things washed up at the seaside are called flotsam. Flotsam that's been thrown from a boat is called jetsam! Some people spend hours 'beachcombing' looking for interesting things – fossils, shells, wooden boxes, treasure . . .

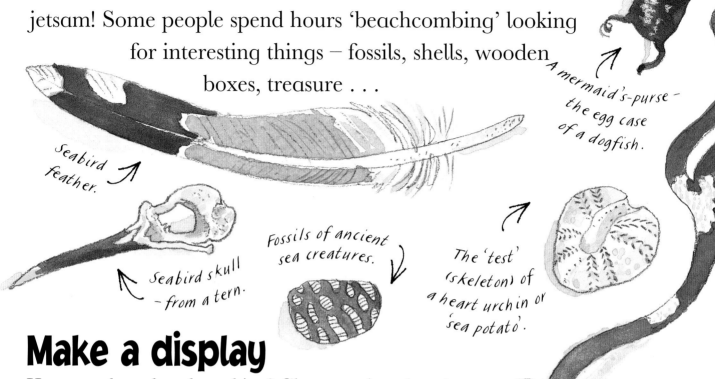

A mermaid's-purse – the egg case of a dogfish.

Seabird feather.

Seabird skull – from a tern.

Fossils of ancient sea creatures.

The 'test' (skeleton) of a heart urchin or 'sea potato'.

Seaweed holdfast.

Make a display

Have you been beachcombing? Choose a clean beach and BE CAREFUL – don't pick up broken glass, old syringes or dirty rubbish. Make a display of your finds.

Dead fish – guzzled by gulls.

Rotting seaweed – eaten by sand hoppers and the maggots of sand-flies.

Sand hoppers and maggots – munched by birds.

Maggot pie!

It's not just us combing the beach – so are lots of animals, but they are searching for food. Nothing is wasted – a dead animal is food for maggots, the maggots are food for larger animals. This linked feeding relationship is called a food chain. Make a maggot pie – now who would like to eat it?

Shells.

Shipworm is a sort of shellfish that burrows into wet wood. It could cause the wooden ships of the past to fall apart.

Bladderwrack seaweed – air bladders help to keep it afloat.

Driftwood that's been eaten by shipworm.

Kelp – a seaweed with long finger-like fronds.

Nylon rope.

Knotted wrack – its yellowy 'fruit' will grow into new seaweed.

Crockery, bottles, tiles – all their edges smoothed by the sea.

Skeleton of a cuttlefish – a type of squid.

1 Choose a smooth piece of driftwood or cardboard as a backing.

2 Stick lumps of paper soaked in PVA glue together on the backing. Push in some feathers. Let it dry.

3 Paint the paper mound pink. When this is dry, spread PVA glue over it and scatter on some dried rice.

4 Imagine this is the carcass of a dead bird on the beach! You've made a really yummy maggot pie for a fox or a gull.

Under the water

When the tide goes out, pools of water are left behind in the sand and rocks. They create a special habitat for many animals, which is fun to explore. But never go rockpooling without asking an adult first.

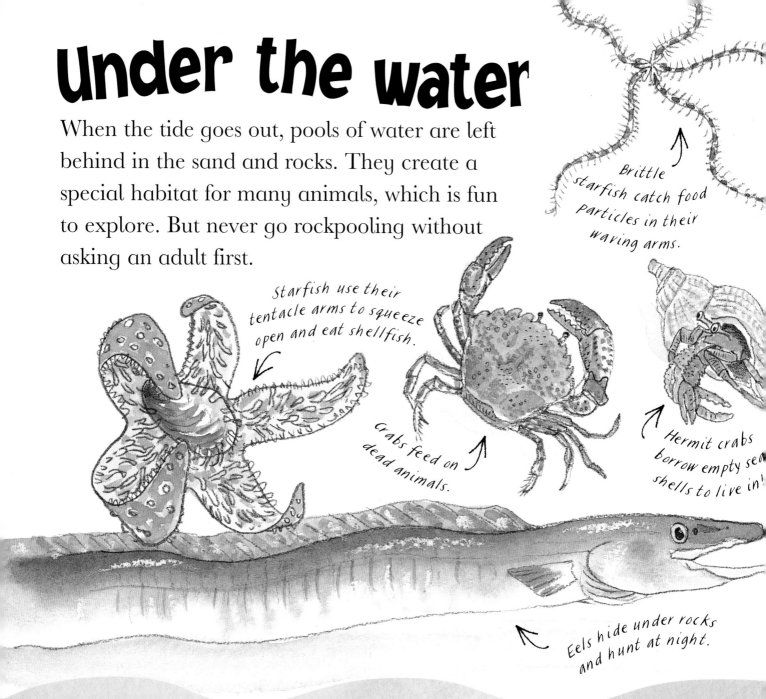

Brittle starfish catch food particles in their waving arms.

Starfish use their tentacle arms to squeeze open and eat shellfish.

Crabs feed on dead animals.

Hermit crabs borrow empty sea shells to live in!

Eels hide under rocks and hunt at night.

Make an aquarium

Sea water animals can't live in ordinary fishtanks – so don't take them home. Try making this instead, it's easier and there is nothing to feed!

1 Cut the top off of a cardboard box and make two 'windows', front and back.

2 Paint the box sea-blue inside. Tape a sheet of bubble wrap over the back window.

3 Draw and cut out some sea creatures. Hang them from sticks that are a little longer than the box.

Shannies peep out from the seaweed they hide in.

Seaweed provides food and shelter.

Prawns are scavengers.

Gobies feed on small shellfish like barnacles.

Lobsters' huge claws crush food and keep danger away!

4 Add strips of sea-coloured bin-liner or tissue paper to the sticks so they hang down like seaweed.

5 Now when it's draughty or you give the sticks a shake, the animals will 'swim' around in your aquarium.

Mermaids and pirates

Long before anyone went to the seaside on holiday, fishermen lived by the sea and survived by catching and selling fish. Other people sailed boats and ships to trade with faraway countries. They faced many dangers, and a few mysteries, on the high seas . . .

Fishy tales!

Many sailors said they had seen mermaids and mermen with long hair and fishy tails. These were really fishy tales – inspired by the seals who swam around the fishing boats.

people from the sea

You can be a mermaid or a merman. Ask a friend to help you make your tail.

1 Wearing a pink or silvery T-shirt, put bubble wrap around your legs and fasten it with packing tape. Shape the foot of the wrap into the tail fins.

2 Decorate your tail with glitter and other sparkly things so it looks scaly.

3 Make yourself a seaweed wig – and a beard if you want – with coloured tissue paper.

Sea monsters

Sailors thought the sea was full of monsters – we still hunt for the Loch Ness monster today. Draw your own sea monster – how scary can you make it?

Bedroom Island Treasure

look under bed for a clue

swivel twice

follow your nose

my brot bedroo

Treasure Map

dunes

beach towel

old log

big stone

sea

Treasure map

Pirates weren't just fishermen's tales. They were real. They robbed ships of their precious cargo. Many pirates buried their treasure on secret islands far out at sea. Invite your friends to a treasure hunt party.

1 **First choose your island – it could be a room in your house or a back garden. Draw a map of your 'island', showing useful landmarks like pieces of furniture, doors or paths.**

2 **Bury or hide some 'treasure' (small toys or sweets) at different places on your island. Mark where you hide each thing on the map. Maybe add a 'key', for example X=Treasure!**

3 **Now put on your pirate clothes, hoist the jolly roger (the skull-and-crossbones flag), give your friends your map and let the treasure hunt begin!**

seaside safety

Sharks are magnificent – and some types can be dangerous when they think swimmers are tasty seal pups! But sharks are rare – there are a lot of other seaside dangers you should be much more careful about.

Dos and Don'ts

• Don't climb on cliffs or explore caves without an adult to supervise you.

• Don't swim unless you're with an adult and don't try to dodge big waves as they break on the beach. They could sweep you away. See the shark bite for more advice about safe swimming.

• Look out for stinging jellyfish and other poisonous beasties, such as weaver fish.

• Wash your hands after a day on the beach – microscopic germs love to live in the sand and sea water at the seaside.

Shipwreck-in-a-jam-jar

If you ever use a boat at the seaside, you have to be extra careful. Sailors can drown if their ship hits rocks in stormy weather. Once a ship is wrecked, it slowly rots and sea animals and plants move in. Make your own shipwreck-in-a-jam-jar.

To the lighthouse!

Lighthouses shine out over the sea and warn sailors of dangerous rocky places. Make your own with a small torch and cardboard tube (a crisp tube is perfect). Make sure the torch fits inside the tube.

Many beaches fly special flags to show if it is safe to swim there. If a red flag is flying, it means it is dangerous – don't swim!

1 Make a rocky base for your lighthouse from Plasticine and surround it with a stormy sea made of scrunched-up tissue paper.

2 Paint the crisp tube red and stick a white strip around its centre.

3 Switch on the torch and slip it upright into the tube.

4 Put a clear plastic cup on top of the lighthouse and attach it on one side so you can still take the torch out to switch your lighthouse on and off.

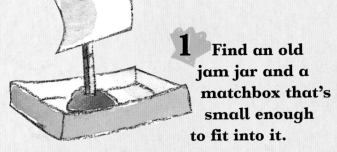

1 Find an old jam jar and a matchbox that's small enough to fit into it.

2 Make the matchbox tray into a boat, using a match for a mast and a paper sail. Stick the mast up with a lump of Plasticine or Blutack. Paint the boat with PVA glue and let it dry.

3 Stick the boat at the bottom of the jar with more Plasticine or Blutack.

4 Add some sand and pebbles around it and fill the jar with clean water.

5 Now you have a seaside souvenir, a variation on a ship-in-a-bottle. How long will your ship last at the bottom of the sea?

pollution is rubbish!

The sea keeps itself clean and the tides clean the coastlines too. But when people leave rubbish on the beach or pollute the sea with sewage or other chemicals, this natural process breaks down, the sea becomes dirty and the life in it begins to die . . .

Oil spills and slicks

Oil spills from tankers are one of the worst kinds of pollution. Oil floats on the surface of the water in a thin 'oil slick' and is dangerous to sea animals in all sorts of ways: it clogs waterproof feathers or fur, letting in water and cold. On the seabed it poisons shellfish, fish and plant life. Try an oil experiment.

1 Fill up a bowl with water. Add 3 drops of cooking oil to the water. The oil floats thinly across the whole surface.

2 Use a small furry toy – or a seabird feather from the beach – to dip on to the surface of your 'slick'. A layer of oil sticks to it – just like it does to a diving seabird when it surfaces in an oil slick.

3 Now put a drop of washing-up liquid on the surface of the oily water. Look what happens! Detergent like washing-up liquid is used to clean oil-covered wildlife.

4 Try washing the feather or toy with washing-up liquid. Notice how wet and soppy it is when you have finished. The liquid takes off the oil but it also washes away natural oils from birds' feathers.

Oiled birds cleaned up at animal rescue centres have to grow new feathers before they can be released safely. Most die before then.

Rubbish

Rubbish is another form of pollution. It can be dangerous, too – plastic multi-pack holders, tin cans, broken glass, old fishing nets can all harm wildlife.

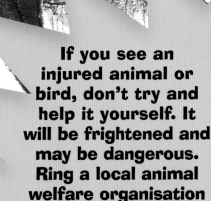

Oiled birds swallow chemicals when they preen.

Oily feathers soak up water – the bird sinks.

It flaps its wings to try to wash, but the oil won't budge.

A gull has got its head stuck in a multi-pack holder.

A gannet has become tangled in a fishing line.

Do a survey

Do a survey of rubbish on a beach. Walk 100 steps along the sand, writing down in a notebook any rubbish you find. You may want to tidy up some of the rubbish you spot but be careful if you do. Some rubbish can have sharp edges or carry nasty germs.

If you see an injured animal or bird, don't try and help it yourself. It will be frightened and may be dangerous. Ring a local animal welfare organisation and they will help.

29

seaside senses

So much to see

For hundreds of years artists, writers and musicians have been inspired by the sea. Write a poem about the things you see at the seaside. What other senses could you use to describe them? Make a rhythm as you sing or speak your poem by clacking two pebbles together.

I must go down to the seas again, to the lonely sea and the sky . . .

from a poem by John Masefield

So much to hear

Listen to the sea and the sounds on the beach . . .
Make a list of what you hear.
Here are some ideas:

Small waves: Splash-splish!
Big waves: Boom! Crash!
Gulls: Ark, ark, ark!
Seaweed: Pop, pop, pop!

Pebble music

'Plip, Plop, Plup!' Lob a handful of small pebbles into the water. What do you hear? Listen how the pebble music changes if you use different sizes or throw lots or just a few in at once, or lob them higher or lower. If you find a flat stone, try to skim it over the surface – how many skims can you do? And what noise does it make as it bounces across the water?

Touch

Collect some seaside objects like smooth pebbles, shells and rubbery seaweed. Sit down in a group in a quiet place. Close your eyes and pass your objects round. Don't look! Just enjoy their lovely shapes and textures.

Smell and taste

One of the first things you notice when you arrive at the sea is the damp, salty smell. You can almost taste it on your tongue! You can find seaside tastes and smells at the supermarket. Next time you are shopping there, spot foods that come from the sea – frozen prawns, fish, sea salt, dried seaweed! Buy some to smell and taste. Write down a list of all the things you see in your notebook and then make a seafood menu. Show it around and see what people like best!

Useful words

Coal The black rock formed over millions of years from dead plants. People burn coal to make heat. Page 6

Driftwood Wood that has floated, or drifted, around on the sea. Pages 7, 15, 18, 19, 21

Dunes Piles of sand blown up by the wind that form beside beaches. Grass usually grows over the dunes. Page 10

Electricity A kind of energy that we use to make many machines work. Pages 9, 14

Erode To break up or wear away rock, stone and soil, usually by the action of wind and water. Page 5

Food chain A group of living things that are linked together because one is eaten by another. Page 20

Force A push or a pull. A force affects the way a thing moves. Pages 8, 10, 14

Gravity An invisible force between two things that pulls them towards each other. The bigger a thing is, the stronger its pull of gravity. We only notice the pull of gravity from something really huge – like the sun, the earth or the moon. Pages 10, 11

Mortar A mixture of cement, sand and water that is used to stick bricks together. Page 7

Pollution Something that makes water and other natural habitats dirty and poisonous, damaging the plants and animals that live there. Pages 28, 29

Rockpools Sometimes called tidepools, these are pools of water that form among rocks or in the sand on a beach at low tide. Page 22

Sandstone A type of rock made by layers of sand pushed together over millions of years. Page 6

Scavenger An animal that eats whatever food scraps it can find, from dead animals to picnic remains. Pages 12, 17, 23

Sewage The dirty water and waste people wash down drains and lavatories. Page 28

Shellfish Sea animals with soft bodies that are protected on the outside by a hard shell. Pages 11, 12, 13, 16, 22, 23, 28

Tide The way the sea level rises and falls two times each day. This movement is caused by the pull of gravity between the moon and the sun and the sea water. Pages 4, 10, 11, 22

UV rays Short for ultraviolet rays. These are rays of light from the sun that we cannot see but they still carry the sun's heat and can damage our skins. Page 15

Volcanic rock Rock made by a volcano when it erupts. Page 6

First published in 2004 by Franklin Watts, 96 Leonard Street, London EC2A 4XD

Franklin Watts Australia, 45-51 Huntley Street, Alexandria, NSW 2015

The illustrations in this book have been drawn by Mick and Brita

Text and illustrations © 2004 Mick Manning and Brita Granström
Editor: Rachel Cooke
Art director: Jonathan Hair

Printed in Hong Kong, China
A CIP catalogue record is available from the British Library.
ISBN 0 7496 5163 6

WELCOME TO THE WORLD, FREJ!